anythink

D0820899

No Longer Property of
ANYTHINK LIBRARIES/
RANGEVIEW LIBRARY DISTRICT

Transportation

Rescue Vehicles

A 4D BOOK

by Mari Schuh

PEBBLE
a capstone imprint

Download the Capstone app!

- Ask an adult to download the Capstone 4D app.
- Scan the cover and stars inside the book for additional content.

When you scan a spread, you'll find fun extra stuff to go with this book! You can also find these things on the web at www.capstone4D.com using the password: rescue.01433

Pebble Books are published by Pebble,
1710 Roe Crest Drive,
North Mankato, Minnesota 56003
www.mycapstone.com

Copyright © 2019 by Pebble, a Capstone imprint.
All rights reserved. No part of this publication
may be reproduced in whole or in part, or stored
in a retrieval system, or transmitted in any
form or by any means, electronic, mechanical,
photocopying, recording, or otherwise, without
written permission of the publisher.

**Library of Congress Cataloging-in-
Publication Data**
Names: Schuh, Mari C., 1975- author.
Title: Rescue vehicles : a 4D book / by Mari Schuh.
Description: North Mankato, Minnesota : Pebble,
a Capstone imprint, [2019] |
  Series: Little pebble. Transportation. | Audience:
  Ages 4–7.
Identifiers: LCCN 2018004152 (print) | LCCN
2018009985 (ebook) | ISBN 9781977101471
(eBook PDF) | ISBN 9781977101433 (hardcover) |
ISBN 9781977101457 (pbk.)

Subjects: LCSH: Emergency vehicles—Juvenile
literature. | Rescue
  Work—Juvenile literature. | CYAC: Rescue work.
| Emergency vehicles. | LCGFT: Picture books. |
Instructional and educational works.
Classification: LCC TL235.8 (ebook) | LCC
TL235.8 .S38 2019 (print) | DDC 629.04/6—
dc23LC record available at https://lccn.loc.
gov/2018004152

Editorial Credits
Karen Aleo, editor; Juliette Peters, designer;
Jo Miller, media researcher;
Kris Wilfahrt, production specialist

Photo Credits
iStockphoto: B&M Noskowski, 5, fabphoto, 17,
FangXiaNuo, 1; Shutterstock: Art Konovalov, 15,
charl898, 21, Jaromir Chalabala, 7, Neil Webster,
9, OgnjenO, 11, Philip Lange, 19, Robert Pernell,
cover

Design Element
Shutterstock: T.Sumaetho

Printed and bound in the United States.
PA021

Table of Contents

Ready to Help

Sirens blast.

Rescue vehicles rush to the scene.

People need help.

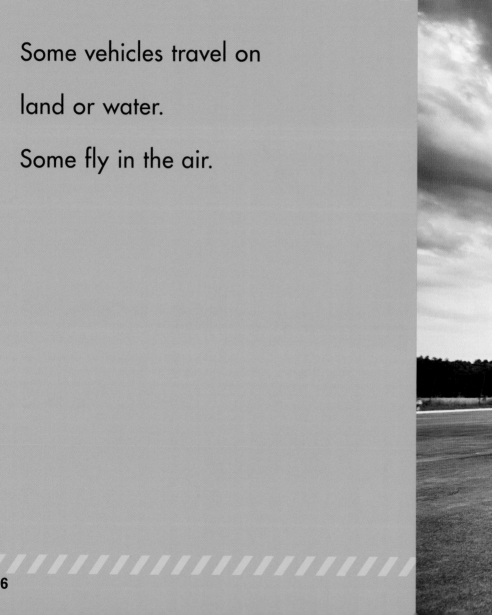

Some vehicles travel on

land or water.

Some fly in the air.

Kinds

Look at the fire truck.

Long hoses help put out fires.

Tall ladders reach people.

Look at the police car.

It is fast!

Police make sure

people obey laws.

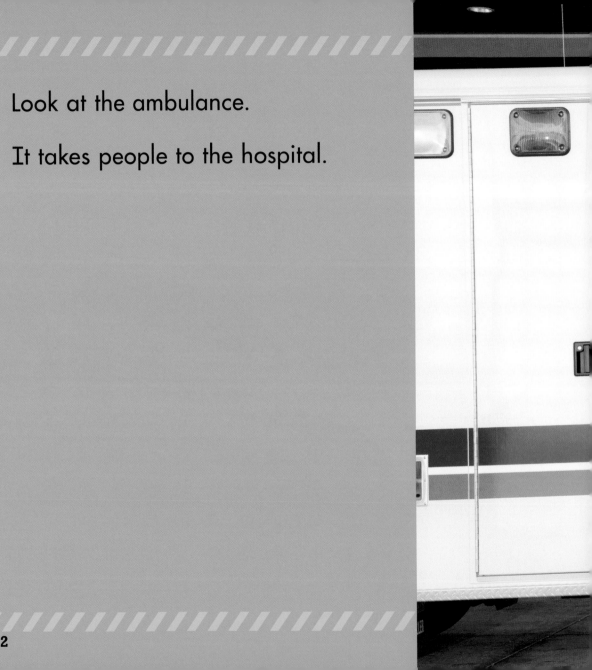

Look at the ambulance.

It takes people to the hospital.

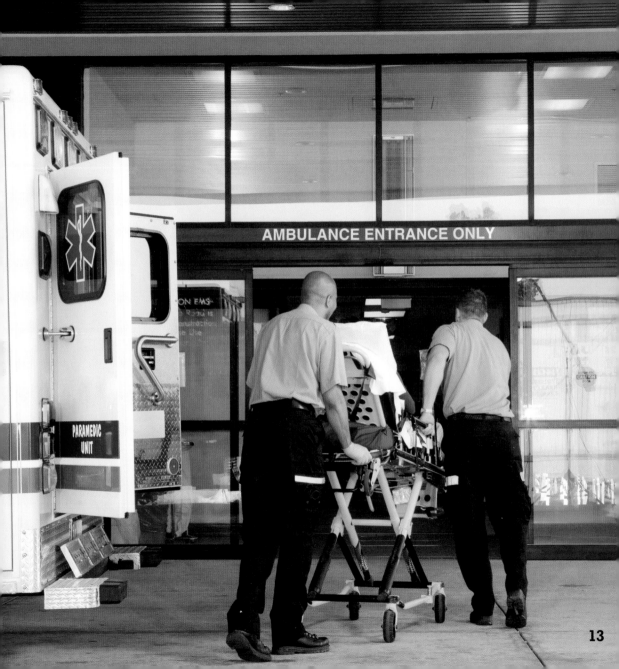

AMBULANCE ENTRANCE ONLY

PARAMEDIC
UNIT

13

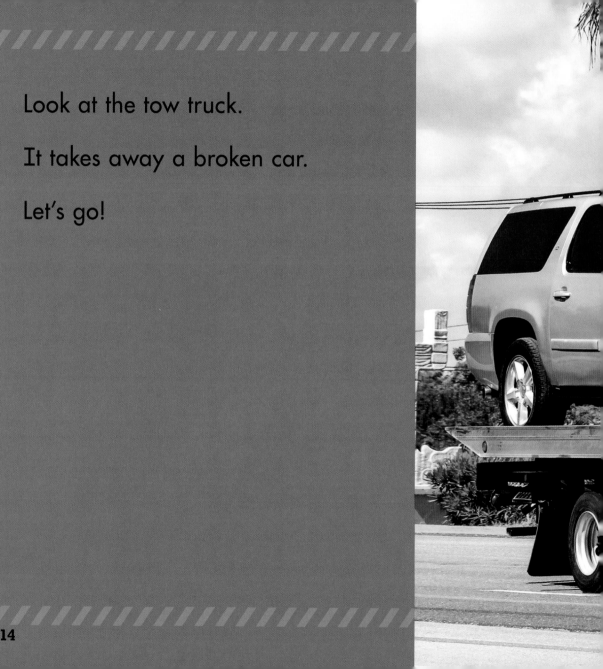

Look at the tow truck.

It takes away a broken car.

Let's go!

15

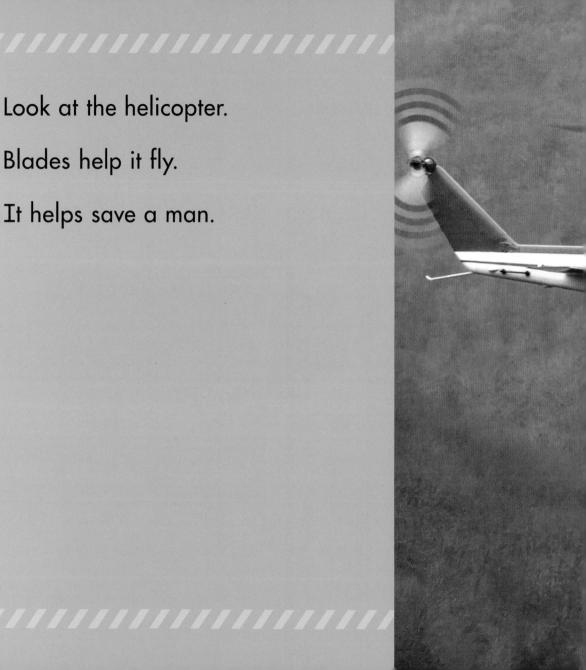

Look at the helicopter.

Blades help it fly.

It helps save a man.

blades

Look at the rescue boat.

It is orange.

The color is easy to see.

Saving Lives

Rescue vehicles save lives.

Help is on the way!

Glossary

ambulance—a vehicle that takes sick or hurt people to a hospital

helicopter—an aircraft that can take off and land in a small space

hospital—a building where doctors and others work to help people who are very sick or badly hurt

obey—to do what someone tells you to do

rescue—to save someone who is in danger

siren—a device that makes a loud sound

vehicle—something used to carry people or things from place to place

Read More

Abramovitz, Melissa. *Emergency Vehicles.* Wild About Wheels. North Mankato, Minn.: Capstone Press, 2015.

Morey, Allan. *Police Cars.* Machines at Work. Minneapolis: Jump!, 2015.

Veitch, Catherine. *Big Machines Rescue!* Big Machines. Chicago: Heinemann Library, 2015.

Internet Sites

Use FactHound to find Internet sites related to this book.

Visit *www.facthound.com*

Just type in 9781977101433 and go.

Check out projects, games and lots more at
www.capstonekids.com

Critical Thinking Questions

1. How do rescue vehicles help people in danger?

2. Name a rescue vehicle that travels on water. Name a rescue vehicle that travels in the air.

3. What kinds of equipment do fire trucks have to help during a fire?

Index